# the
# mermaid's
# voice
# returns
# in
# this
# one

# the mermaid's voice returns in this one

## amanda lovelace

Andrews McMeel
PUBLISHING®

for the little bookmad girl.
thank you for deciding to
live long enough
to see yourself
write a book.
then another.
then another.
then another.

# contents

When I think of *The Little Mermaid*, there are two narratives that come to mind: the dark and twisted fairy tale penned by Hans Christian Andersen and the nostalgic Disney rendition from my childhood. In this gorgeous collection of poetry, amanda lovelace has brought these two alternate worlds seamlessly together. The mermaid gets her voice back, and she does so with a vengeance.

As a writer, the words you put down on paper are synonymous with your voice. There was a time in my life when I stopped writing. For years, I ignored my words. I'd lost my voice. I'd lost myself.

But the world works in mysterious ways. It yearns to remind you of your place and purpose.

At first, this reminder will appear as a gentle tap on your shoulder. But if you don't pay attention, it will come in the most brutal fashion.

And that is what happened to me. My life stopped. My world came crashing down. And when there was nothing left, my words came back to me. My voice came back. And with that voice, I rebuilt my life, from the ground up.

Now, years later, I am proud to join amanda and a collective of fresh voices, some of whom you will meet in this book. We come from all over the world, refusing to settle for the narrative that has been written for us time and time again. We are writing our own alternate endings. This is our time. This is our revolution. Pick up a pen and join us.

xo Lang

warning I:

this is not
a mermaid's ~~tail~~ tale.

there is no
sea-maiden.

there is no
sea-sky.

there are no
sea-stars.

there is no
sea-song.

what there is,
however,

is the story
of how

they tried
to quiet her

& how her screams
dismantled

the moon.

warning II:

only mending
ahead.

## swan song I

i'm dousing
my fire.

i'm dropping
my sword.

i'm melting
my crown.

i'm destroying
my castle

& then i'm
hurling it

straight
into that

perilous
sea.

all
this time,

i thought
myself

a motherfucking
queen,

&
only now

am i
realizing

that it was
all make-believe.

# swan song II

i have a
        terrible habit
of writing
        myself
braver than
        i'll ever be,
& i'm not sure
        which of us
i'm trying
        to convince—
you, or
        me.

you are
the chapter
                    *i didn't*

know
if i should
                    *tell*

for the fear
that i would
someway,
somehow
write you
back into
the current
chapter
of
my story.

in one of our many worlds existed a girl who couldn't handle how very sad & confusing life could be, so she approached one of her many overstuffed bookshelves, got up on her tippy-toes, & pleaded to the dozens of warped & well-loved spines, "i want nothing more in this world than to be one of you." miraculously, the books listened. they more than listened. from that day on, they took her in & raised her as one of their own. each night while she was supposed to be sleeping, the girl's new family scribbled her into fairy tales about princesses & witches & even her favorite fantastical creature: mermaids.

# in a distant land . . .

# I. the sky

"

*after the*
*unimaginable*
*happened,*
*the mermaid*
*left the*
*dried up sea*
*of*
*her planet*
*& rode*
*a shooting star*
*straight into*
*the sky.*

~~door~~
~~sealed.~~

~~television~~
~~off.~~

~~curtains~~
~~closed.~~

~~hammering~~
~~heart.~~

~~creaking~~
~~bed.~~

~~tear-filled~~
~~silence.~~

~~years~~
~~shattered.~~

*- a little girl played hide & seek in the wrong place.*

how he
managed
to choke
me
with
both of his
wrists
ribboned
together
behind his
back.

- *"do not say a word."*

there
was

                *nothing*

i
could
have
done.

there
was

                *no one*

i
could
have
told.

*- a pebble i cannot get down.*

what felt like
hours of

begging
& screaming

&
crying

& shouting
"don't you love me?"

was
wiped clean

with
a single word

from your
mouth.

by
some miracle,

you
convinced

my
mother

that
it was okay

if i took
my bike out

into
the rain

&
rode

to
my heart's

content—
because

if
anyone

could be
trusted

to
turn back

from
danger,

it was
me,

- *wasn't it?*

it
should
be safe
for little girls
~~to ride their~~
~~little yellow~~
~~bikes~~
~~around~~
~~the block~~
~~without~~
~~someone~~
~~ending up~~
~~in~~
~~handcuffs.~~

- *wanted.*

"call me dad,"
he would tell me.

i wanted
so badly
to tell him
"no"
because
i already had one
& he could
never hope
to measure
up.

- *you weren't family by blood or the family i chose.*

when
i cannot
cope
i
erase
it
instead.

*- not a printing error.*

star light,

       star bright,

first star

       i see tonight;

i wish i may,

       i wish i might

flee my skin

       for but a night.

- *bibliophile.*

"i wish i could be her friend,"
the girl whispers
down into the
tear-stained pages,
lovingly caressing
the gold-dipped edges.

"no—i'd rather *be* her."

- *ariel.*

"i wish i could be her friend,"
the fictional girl echoes back.
she reaches up,
her hand falling back
down to her side when
she realizes her mistake.

"no—i'd rather *be* her."

- *ariel II.*

&
that's
how
the girl
learned
how to love


but only ever
from a great
distance.

sometimes
she cannot
tell the
difference

between

the days
she's walked
this earth
as herself

&

the days
she's walked
through paragraphs
as someone else.

*- no one noticed & she liked it that way.*

do you
ever
find
yourself
nostalgic
for

the life

you never
got to
have?

- *(because i do.)*

do you
ever
find
yourself
nostalgic
for
                        the person
you never
got to
be?

*- (because i do II.)*

whenever
you need
a healthy
dose
of serenity,

crawl
through
the frosted
windowpane
of her mind.

blades
of grass grow
in shades
of
paradise.

opals
droop from
branches
instead of
leaves.

rivers
flow with
undiluted
rosebud
water.

milk&honey
falls from
the clouds
instead of
rain.

even the
absolutely
unthinkable
happens
here:

children
learn peacefully,
unafraid of
angry hands
around guns.

*- hooks encrusted in sand.*

though
i tend to believe

poppies
probably

speak
in secret,

i'm under
no illusion

that
you will ever

read
this poem

or
any other.

(you
lie still

beneath
the headstone

i placed my
lipstick palm on.)

still,
i cannot rest

until
i write

these
words

down
for you:

i'm
nobody.

i'm
nobody, too.

- *called back.*

(homage to the poem "I'm Nobody! Who are you?"
by Emily Dickinson)

when i tell you i'm still waiting for my hogwarts letter, what i mean to say is i never meant to be here for so long.

*- forever wandering lost & wandless.*

"maybe
i'm not
the book you
dog-ear &
keep with you
always,"

the girl
murmured,
pulling her
sleeves
over her
hands.

"maybe
i'm the book
you forget
to bookmark
& leave
on the train."

- *shrinking violets like us.*

can't

      a prince
      a princess
      a n y o n e

just
come along
& gaze
upon me
with such
adoration
it's
as if i'm
the gem
of the deep,
not the rubble
of pompeii?

- *when will it be my turn?*

in
search
of someone

who
made
her feel like

she belonged
in this
world,

she
went on
countless

      journeys
      expeditions
      voyages.

*- it was always the girl through the looking glass.*

she didn't kiss frogs.
she kissed great white sharks.

i find that
losing
yourself
in love letters
& white lies
& time differences
& dropped signals
is
always easier
than
venturing out
into
the unpredictable

- *wild.*

the prince
of her dreams
was sipping
on an
old-fashioned

while
she popped
lotus
blossoms
into her mouth.

neither
of them felt
their vices
were quite
doing the trick,

so
they left
them
behind
& ran away.

it
didn't matter
where
they
ended up,

so long as
it was away.
so long as
it was
together.

happenstance
/ˈha-pən-stans/
*noun*

    1: he & i.
    2: me, falling down those treetop
    eyes.

*- who was i before you?*

"i ought to let you know—
i find my prince
every year,"

- *i said.*

"then
this year—
this year will be all mine,"

*- he replied, unfazed.*

the
very minute

he
realized

he
could

wrap
his fingers

around
my wrists

with
space left

&
fill in

the dips
between

my
hipbones

with
handfuls

of
stones

&
seashells,

he
made

for
damn sure

my
plate was

always
overflowing.

- *filed under: things i hate that i owe to you.*

you
weren't
the first one
to tell me
they would

kiss
*my scars*
*so pretty,*

but
you were
certainly
the first
i believed.

*- now i know you can't fix someone else.*

everything started to make sense once i learned that you don't need to be caught underneath an ill-tempered wave in order to drown. i'm talking about how it feels when your fingers are twisted up in my long, blackwater hair, pulling just enough to hurt. pulling just enough for me to not want you to stop.

- *dry drowning.*

i don't mean
to frighten you,
but i would
seriously
consider
drinking
the atlantic whole
if only you
asked me
to.

*- what wouldn't i do for you?*

i wish you had been my first love.
i would have even settled for second love.

- *third is the ~~worst~~ best.*

shiny gold flecks coat the tips of my fingers the first time i place them onto your skin. bringing them to my lips, i cannot help but to think that it tastes like something not of this world. carelessly, i misplace the age-old fairy lore which warns humans like me never to eat or drink anything that seems too good to be real, lest you lose yourself too completely.

*- my midas.*

you're
the kind of
intriguing
that
inspired
thousand-page
epics.

- *how many centuries have you lived?*

finding
a way to fit
into your
sun-kissed
arms
was almost
excruciatingly
easy.

*- you were always my favorite wreck.*

each morning before school, my mother did not feed me breakfast. she fed me wisdom. first, she brushed my hair with a fork. soon after, braids fell to my waist as she kissed the top of my head, whispering against it, "now. don't you dare lean out your window & let it all fall down. you never know who will show up & climbclimbclimb on up. heed my advice: even villains will go all dizzy & heart-eyed for you. do not ever become fooled by such trickery."

- *mother knows best.*

# II. the shipwreck

"

*but the stars—*
*they see*
*everything & are*
*loyal to no one.*
*when she*
*whispered*
*her wishes*
*into them,*
*the voices from*
*her nightmares*
*came crashing*
*down.*

problem
is,
some
people
are living,
breathing

I C E B E R G S

just
waiting
for the
perfect moment
to pull you
under.

- *titanic.*

swallowing
the memories
is like
biting down

on
a mouthful
of
sea glass—

the iron
filling up
~~my~~ her
throat

is the
only way
she knows
she's still

alive.

- *try as i may, i keep spitting you up.*

the first time you take me home & introduce me to your parents, your father takes one look at me & says, "that girl looks like she's much too smart for her own good."

- *why wasn't i smart enough to stay away from you?*

a smile.
irresistible lashes.
a dark room.
legs tangled.
peace.

- *this is how i'd like to remember you.*

he
told me
he was
fond

of
broken
girls
like me

&
i
didn't
so much

as
blink
an
eye.

later,
i thought
to
myself,

*if only*
*they had*
*taught*
*me*

*how to*
*recognize*
*the warning*
*flares*

*instead*
*of*
*wasting*
*their time*

*teaching*
*me*
*how*
*to*

*mistake*
*them*
*for*
*flattery.*

with
his
pocketknife,

he
sheared off
~~my~~ her hair

while
she slept
curled

as
a quiet
comma

into
his
side,

only
for him
to

glue it
all back
to the ends

so
he could
show her

everything
he could do
to her

&
still
manage

to
get away
with it.

*- maleficent.*

he
~~held~~
~~her hand.~~

he
~~grabbed~~
~~her breast.~~

he
~~turned~~
~~off the light.~~

he
~~walked~~
~~her to his bed.~~

he
~~laid~~
~~her down.~~

he
~~tore~~
~~her shirt.~~

he
~~told her~~
~~he loved her.~~

he
~~shoved his~~
~~tongue inside.~~

~~he said~~
~~he wanted~~
~~to marry her.~~

~~he~~
~~placed his~~
~~hand between.~~

~~he~~
~~kissed across~~
~~her collarbone.~~

~~he~~
~~sobbed~~
~~onto her cheeks.~~

*- he split ~~my~~ her tail in two.*

no matter
how hard i

*scrub*
*scrub*
*scrub,*

you're
still
everywhere
i don't
want you
to be.

did she, in her last waking moments, forgive him, or was she secretly sending her curses to the gods who did not let the roof collapse on the notches of her beloved's traitorous spine, even if it proved fatal for them both?

- *desdemona.*

(homage to the play *Othello* by William Shakespeare)

she's come to the conclusion that they like her because she's sad & even more so because she's quiet. it's a lethal combination that makes it impossible for her to tell them:

*- stop. / no. / don't.*

i
acquired
a gift
for living
outside of
                    myself
whenever
i needed
to swim
away
from you.

*- mermaid escapist III.*

how he
managed
to choke
me
with
both of his
wrists
roped
together
behind his
back.

- *"i know you wanted it."*

how she
managed
to choke
me
with
both of her
wrists
vined
together
behind her
back.

- *"but you didn't say no, right?"*

the day
i handed you
my
ever-glowing
heart,
i
did not
hand you
anything
else.

- *on being called a tease.*

you still watch me while i'm driving & i still pretend i don't notice you watching. you still hold my hand & i still hold yours right back. you still tell me that you love me & i still tell you that i love you, too. we still kiss when we think no one else is watching, secretly hoping that they are. we even still go for hot coffee when it's a hundred & two degrees outside. we pretend until our teeth disintegrate & our gums bleed from the effort it takes to smile it all away.

*- trying to keep my eyes on the road.*

what
if
he
just
does it
to another
girl?

*- this is why i can't go.*

some days, i still want to believe we can traipse into the forest & come across an enchanted pocket watch that will take us back in time to erase it all & start from scratch.

*- this isn't that kind of fairy tale.*

cages

are
still cages

even
when they're

designed
to

look
just like

castles.

- *illusionist.*

at
this point,
staying
with you
is nothing
more
than
muscle
memory.

an
apology
has
never
known
the walls
of your
mouth.

- *how can you just walk away?*

we
put on
a hell
of a show,
but
the curtains—
they
cannot hide
the history
of you.

*- this cannot go on.*

&
one day,

you were
nowhere

to be found
anymore.

i swear,
i ran to the edge

of
every cliff

just to prove it
to myself.

it
was as if

the wind
simply

did
away with you

like it does
with

plastic
shopping bags

& remainders
of autumn,

sweeping
you up

like it
didn't just

take
away

every
last ounce

of
proof

of
what

you did
to me.

- *i wondered if you were a changeling, except
  someone forgot to replace you.*

some
stories
don't have
happy
endings.

some
stories
don't have
endings
at all.

       ours didn't.

          ours couldn't.

       ours won't.

it was
easier
to
pretend
you died.

it was
easier
to kill the
sleeping
prince.

- *i wrote my own ending in blood.*

give me lavender. give me valerian. give me warmed milk. give me the sound of every raindrop to ever slide down the side of the earth. yes, i will still have trouble falling asleep. because of you, i've never been able to see a bed as a place of rest—only unrest. even when my bones & my eyelids beg for sweet mercy, the second my head hits my pillow, something in the back of my mind will always be trying to remind me of those moments when i learned that sex & violence are not the same thing.

- *unsleeping beauty.*

you do not have
a bed anymore;
you only have
a casket.

*- why do i find no relief in this?*

the heaviness of your hips
never goes

- *phantom.*

he sort of
looks like you,
but i know he
can't be you—

not unless
dead men
have learned
to walk.

he
just has
that long stride
about him—

that
mischievous
wide-eyed look
about him—

that
laugh—
my god, that apocalyptic
laugh about him—

& the family
of cicadas
nesting
in my lungs

cannot
listen to
logic
or reason

because
when it
comes
to you,

i've only
ever had
the chance

to                                    t.
teach them              h
fight or          g

              l      i
     -f

you stopped
leaving bruises
around my neck
so i started
leaving them
everywhere
else.

- *bookends & knuckles.*

every
touch
that comes
in sequel to
y  o  u  r  s
feels like   a
grenade.

*- tick, tick, . . . boom!*

i want
to believe
that
most people
mean no harm
to others.

that
not everyone
is capable
of the
same things
you were.

that
someone can
touch me
& do it
out of
tenderness.

- *sometimes we have to feed ourselves lies*
  *just to live.*

will i have to spend the afterlife
finding ways to hide from you?

on the weekends, my mother used to drive my sister & me down to the beach, though she so rarely liked to get in & swim.

instead, she would take each of our hands & lead us just a few shallow steps into the water—only up to our ankles. she would say to us, "stand still & wait for the next wave to roll in, then close your eyes. when it drifts back out, it will feel like it's taking you along with it. don't worry, though. i won't let anything happen to you, my babies. it's perfectly okay to let go."

sometimes, i want to be able to let go like that again, except for the part where i open my eyes & i'm disappointed to find that i haven't been carried far, far, far away from here.

*- a mermaid escapist IV.*

mostly, i just want to know what it's like to feel something between elation & despair, besides nothing at all.

none of my
favorite songs
sound quite
the same
in your wake.

where
there was
once
a glorious
orchestra,

there's
nothing
except doom
& screeching
violins.

- *kill the conductor.*

"when
our villains
win,
do not fret.
just
rewrite
the story."

- *mother knows best II.*

# III. the song

"

&
so
she did
what any
rational woman
would do—
ever so calmly,
she reached out
& she tore
the stars
apart.

i watched
you watching me
wane. now, you have
no fucking choice
other than to
watch me

*- become full.*

becoming
your
own
savior
sometimes
means
knowing
when
you
need to
ask for
help.

*- therapy session no. 1.*

i refuse
to
believe
you took
something
irreplaceable
from me
in
that
moment.

*- i still have every part of myself.*

I. when they say "no."
II. when they can't say "no."

*- they're both assault.*

you
don't
get to say
it's
my fault
for
staying.

it's
his fault
for
making me
afraid to
stay
or go.

the
first person
who touched me
was not my
first.

- *i'm deciding my firsts from now on.*

&

i want to
take you to the bay
where i was raised

&

watch
the sky fade from
blue to orange to pink

&

show you
where i swam
as a child

&

i want to
rest my head
on your shoulder

when

i ask you if
we'll see each other
in the life after this one

because

i know none of this
would happen in
this life

since

you
were the lesson
that made me realize

redemption

is not a thing
that washes up
on shore.

no—

not
in this life,
no.

*- not in any life, lovely.*

the
only way
i can
foresee
surviving
you
is by
finding
that place
between
forgiving
& forgetting,
if it even
exists.

- *this is how i choose to douse my fire.*

this is me
pressing
my finger
to the sand,

delicately
drawing
your name
there,

& then
stepping back
so i can
watch

you
as you're
finally
carried away.

- *goodbye.*

i don't write
what i write
to hurt you.

- *i write what i write*
*to heal me.*

an update for the girl i used to be:

we live in a tiny apartment near the
sea now. it has a desk for us to write
on. it has heat to warm us. it has food
for us to eat. it has a friendly ghost. it
has a caring spouse & a playful kitten
who brightens all our days. we have
everything we need & everything we
never thought we could have. fighting
your way here was well worth it. don't
give it all up yet.

the first night
in our new place,

i spilled
a glass of water

on the
kitchen floor.

the second night
in our new place,

i spilled
a glass of water

on the
living room rug.

jokingly,
i said to him,

"i guess
our home

is
blessed

with
good luck now."

what i meant
to say is,

"i'm so sorry
i can't touch anything

without
immediately

finding
a way to

tarnish
it

before it
tarnishes me."

what i should
have said is,

"i'm sorry,
i'm sorry."

- *"i'm but a work in progress."*

he
immediately
lowers
his umbrella

when i say
i've never
been kissed
in the rain,

&

by
some
kind of
miracle,

his kiss
does not
feel like
a grenade.

*- the good kind of drowning.*

scene:

>     you,
>     grabbing
>     for my wrist,
>     locking eyes
>     with me over
>     your shoulder
>     while we run
>     for the last train
>     headed home
>     with hundreds
>     of faceless people
>     rushing up
>     behind us
>     so they won't
>     have to
>     stand.

*- i don't mind standing if i'm standing next to you.*

*he exists.*

therefore,
i know
for a fact
that
humanity
is not
dissolving
before
my
eyes.

when i was too frightened to take the plunge, you were the one who told me it was time to take a chance, that i was spending too many years reading about the grand adventures of fictional people & never trying to live them myself. nowadays, we may be strangers who only nod "hello" to each other across crowded rooms, but i'll never forget what you did for me in that moment. thank you for seeing the potential in me, because now i finally see all the possibilities that were lying dormant in me, too.

*- for my childhood friend.*

in one world, romeo doesn't drink the poison. juliet doesn't pierce herself. instead, they decide to drink wine until they fall asleep messily in each other's arms. the next morning, they wake up hungover, nursing killer headaches as they take on the world as well as their families. everything turns out just fine.

- *i believe in endless worlds.*

in the next world, romeo & juliet end up together again. they have a grand wedding surrounded by their family & friends, who all have a hand on the hilt of their sword, but everything is okay because at least no one dies. on their wedding night, juliet is terrified to tell romeo that she wants to kiss him but she doesn't want to sleep next to him. in the same world, romeo doesn't hesitate a single second before he tells her that it's okay, he understands. he will stay with her no matter what she wants or doesn't want.

*- he will stay by her side even if she never wants to sleep next to him.*

in another world, romeo & juliet make it out alive, except they don't end up together in the end. hold on, though, because it's not a tragic ending. they eventually part ways, forever remaining the best of friends, travelling through eras we haven't yet seen until romeo can hold hands with a boy & juliet can hold hands with a girl without fear hanging over their heads.

- *i believe in endless worlds III.*

i am magic
all the days i am
a woman
& i am magic
all the days i am
not.

- *demigirl / demigoddess.*

i
tucked
my story
into
the folds
of silence
in
order
to put
other
people
at ease.

- *no more.*

i
painted
my trauma
in shades of
crown gold
& marigold pink
to
make it
pretty
enough
to be enjoyed
by others.

*- no more II.*

for the first time in months, i wake up feeling okay. i don't waste my morning setting alarm after alarm & turning back over, blinds & eyelids shut to the promise of the new day, to the quickly approaching afternoon.

i roll out, stretching my laced fingers toward the ceiling, the smallest of grins beginning to grow on my face.

*maybe i can be happy,* i think.

*or maybe i can't,* i think.

i quickly shake the thought from my head, humming a wordless tune i picked up from an old music box in the attic. sometimes it's necessary to shut down the little voice that tells me this is but a rare, short-lived moment before i become someone entirely unrecognizable from the person i woke up as.

in all reality, there's a very good chance tonight won't be okay.

but right now,

things are good.

*- that's all i need for now.*

i've always fancied myself a mermaid of sorts. i must confess that i haven't swam since long before i started punishing my body for all the things that were never its fault.

this whole time, i've been covering up these arms that embrace & these legs that carry because i was always petrified of the damage the lightning storm scars would cause. i imagined birds flocking to safety. i imagined deer sprinting back into the shelter of the wood. i imagined children rushing for their parents' bedrooms.

yes, it's true.

lightning can & does kill.

once, it crept through the window & took the baby girl i share generations of blood with.

i've also learned that lightning kills the thing that stops trees from bursting through the soil & giving life back to me.

- *every day is an act of survival.*

on one of my palms, my lifeline stops short. on the other palm, my lifeline dips precariously into my marked-up wrist. i'm not sure which one of them is telling the truth, & part of me never wants to know. the only thing i can do is learn to live with the idea that i will never be cured. i will always be in the process of healing.

- *making the most of it.*

i thought my world was coming to a crashing end, & maybe it did, in some manner of speaking. in the process, photographs fell off the wall, & i still find pieces of glass stuck in the sunken wooden stairs. small cracks formed in some parts of my foundation. in every room, if you place a glass marble in the middle of the floor, it will roll along where the floorboards tilt unevenly. some doors stick & some doors open all by themselves when you walk by them.

the house still stands, though.

it still stands.

*- a home without character isn't a home.*

i fill
my plate
up
& then
i empty it
again.
these days,
it's all for
me.

*- i am my reason for recovery.*

today,
i love the way
i look in
my sundress
& it's not
because
someone else
convinced
me to.

- *i am my reason for recovery II.*

I. breathe.
II. charge my crystals.
III. collect seashells.
IV. write a little each day.
V. take more bubble baths.
VI. say "hello" to the fairies.
VII. drink more spearmint tea.
VIII. re-read my favorite fairy tales.
IX. let no one invalidate me.
X. give myself time.

*- i vow to.*

a victim

or a survivor?

a victim

or a survivor?

a victim

or a survivor?

- *i have settled on both.*

the
further along
i come,
the more
i'm
beginning
to
realize that
maybe—
just
maybe—
there is
such
a thing
as fate.
as destiny.

if
after
everything
i'm
still
breathing,
then
there must
be
a reason
even
if
i
haven't
seen it
yet.

most stories
don't have
a clear,
defined message.
they aren't
supposed to.
we must
take
the good
with the bad
with the grey
&
decide
what
we want
to do
with it
all.

- *i'm still alive & therefore so is hope.*

the night
may fall,
but
i will
always
remain.

- *i'm my own sunset.*

the dawn
may break,
but
i will
always
reign.

- *i'm my own sunrise.*

for
our
assignment,
we had to
take ourselves
out on a date.

i went to
a flower shop
named
*in the garden*
& bought
myself

a
bouquet
of
wilting daisies
everyone else
turned down

&
i
attached
a love note
from myself
to read later.

i
went up
the street to
*water witch coffee*
& picked up
two danishes

only
i would be
eating,
&
before dinner,
no less.

i made
a pot of coffee
big enough for four
& i stood outside,
mug perched
in hand,

staring
into the thin,
winter-bare
forest
in my
backyard.

for
what,
i must admit
i'm not
entirely
certain.

i'm
no longer
searching
for reasons
or explanations
for the past.

i'm
only
searching
for breadcrumbs
leading to
more breadcrumbs

that will,
with any
luck,
eventually
lead me
down

the path
i've been looking
for
this whole
time.

- *homeward.*

"be
stronger
than the
villains.
be every
storybook
heroine
come to life."

- *mother knows best III.*

# IV. the surviving

"

*a chorus of*
*mermaids*
*cried*
*out to her then,*

*'DON'T BE AFRAID*
*TO SING.*

*BELT IT OUT.*

*YOUR VOICE*
*COULD SINK SPACESHIPS.'*

when
you've walked
on
daggers
your
entire life,
you don't
even know
how
to trust
the softness
of
sand
between
your toes.

*- but you need to try anyway.*

I say I want your fingers
in my mouth

I say I want your fingers
in my hair

I say I want the violent
slide of your tongue
like a blade across my throat

You say
haven't you done this before?

Hasn't he touched you
like this before?

Girl, don't you know
it's not supposed to hurt?

I press my mouth
to the wound
Until it
disappears

I say
I know
I know

Do you?
Do you?

- *blade.*
by caitlyn siehl

you have been known
to get cut by
your own hand
& others'.

you have been known
to pry the scabs open,
bleed them
out.

you have been known
to rub them in
with dirt &
grime.

yesterday,
they were
angry scarlet
gashes.

today,
they are
quietly fading
hairlines.

tomorrow,
tomorrow—

- *you'll just have to wait around & see.*

I need you to know
I loved him enough
to lie to everyone who knew me
about how bad it got.

I need you to know
there is still a bullet
lodged between my ribs
in the shape of his holy mouth.

I need you to know
the night the neighbors saw
what they did, when I took
back my voice

finally found the strength
to call him a monster,
I woke up the next morning
and I did not feel brave.

I woke up feeling
like the love of my life

      is a monster

which is the opposite of triumph.

Which is the whole world
Dropped. Clattering
across the hardwood floor.

We talk about survival
like it's a thing that makes you
stronger.

Like it is a lesson learned.
As if it does not steal your truth
fashion it into a killing machine.

As if a thing that does not kill you
makes you more than a person
who is not killed.

But I remember
I remember everything.
I was a bird before this.

Now,
a graveyard
of the unburied.

My healing is ugly.
My edges cracked and uninspiring.

But still, they are my edges.
Still, I am healing.

Isn't that itself a song?
A chorus of rage and gentle

worthy of a dance.

Say Survivor.

Say it with its whole
unbearable weight.

and say it again.

and say amen.

Say amen.

- *notes on the term survivor.*
by clementine von radics

like you were nothing more than an overgrown wildflower field, this foul world took a hatchet to you. painted your petals in shades of grey when they were always supposed to be in blaring neon. collected your sunflowers & tulips in bouquets with the roots hanging down, dripping away with the thing that once held them together at the root. shoved them in your face & had the nerve to act as though they were a gift to bestow, not a thing for you to mourn. be comforted by the knowledge that the wind already blew your seeds away to be planted as far as the eye can see.

- *there always exists more than one opportunity for you to grow.*

trauma didn't change you all at once
it carved slowly every day
like rivers do
it was patient while it hollowed you out

so it's a sculptor or it's a knife
you take your pain and you other it
you give it a new name
and a new face

you say *this might have helped shape me*
*but it is not a part of me*

you say *i meant to break open*
*to make room for stars*

*- untitled.*
by trista mateer

little alice may have done a freefall through all of time & space, but that doesn't mean you have to jump off the bridge after her. sometimes the best thing you can do for yourself is to let the past remain in the past. darling, *shhh*—it was never as pretty as you like to pretend it was. it's time you give your present a fair chance. after all, it's never once given up on you.

- *don't touch the stones.*

healing is a journey.
sometimes the type
you jump into the
ocean and swim
across for.

maybe your journey to
healing doesn't have
to be like a fire where
you burn yourself at
the stake and drag
your feet through
hot coals, skinning
yourself bare for
everyone to see.

let the waves of
self-reflection
take you in.

wade in your honesty,
your strength, your
b r a v e r y .

we survived our abuse,
now swim.

- *wading.*
by gretchen gomez

someone mistreats you again & you reply the same way you always do ("oh, it's alright. i'm used to it by now.") before looking down at your shoes. it's there that i will write an invisible reminder to you: don't ever take anyone's bullshit. if they treat you as anything less than royalty, then show them exactly what a mermaid-witch-queen like yourself can accomplish.

*- slay those dragons II.*

i. i still search the sky for clues that could lead me back to you, but i promise that the days of concentrated star-gazing are long gone. in their place lie mornings where i look to my feet and the earth beneath them, how they sink into the soil. the comfort of my roots helps me believe that healing is not just around the corner, it is happening with every breath to depart my blessed body.

ii. my low days are frequent and stubborn, but eventually, my eyes will stop burning. they will transform from red to gleaming, hungry for the very things you could never offer. that is when i will remember who i am and what i have outgrown. your confines were destined to suffocate me at one point or another. all i have to do is discover the courage to punch through its low ceilings and narrow corridors.

iii. when our blazing empire fell, i held a funeral for the ash. believe me, you did not disappear unnoticed. battles were fought howling your name. with every sword unsheathed, i expected to hear your voice persuading me to return. but i let a moment pass. (on the worst days, i had to let several moments pass.) when silence settles in, peace follows. when i am aware of peace, i remind myself to stay focused. i must transcend you.

iv. i am coming to terms with the way your grasp pulls me in and returns me to a path upon which we once walked together. i am also learning to accept that, while you will always sprint for the ocean, i will forever remain an earth sign.

- *earth / water.*
by noor shirazie

the
beloved
will
always fall.
they're
the world's
darling,
glittery things
until
someone
strolls
up to them
&
tells them
they
no longer are.

- *alas, your scraped knees will always mend.*

you are so much more
than the rippling fallacies
your reflection whispers to you.

those demons that lurk beneath the surface
do not know you
even though they pretend to.

and someday,
though it feels impossible,
you will see yourself as i do.

when time has finally finished healing your scars,
your siren call will scream "I AM GOOD ENOUGH!"
and even your bewitching smile will shine through.

but until that day, the day you are okay,
just keep singing yourself to sleep,
and eventually your monsters will stop haunting you.

- *trust me.*
by jenna clare

you are sad now.
you are not sad forever.

there are no paved roads
to healing.

you must build one
brick by brick.

there will be backtracks
before breakthroughs but—

you must collapse
into yourself
before rebuilding.

you must unearth
every wound
before learning
the power of salt.

you will build
that yellow brick road—

in your own time and
on your own terms.

- *the grit of healing.*
by ky robinson

nearly an entire year goes by where you're puddle jumping & thinking, *well, i suppose it could be much worse than this,* & then suddenly it's hurricane season from june through november. some years, it's all downpour. some years, it's all drizzle. others, there's not even a single drop. there's no telling what's in store for you, or when you'll feel like you must pack up your crown & stick it underneath your bed, waiting patiently for the day when you believe you're worthy of adorning it.

*- rare as those days can be, they do always come.*

the last time you were asked for forgiveness,

you had the same dream every night.
no, not a dream, a nightmare,
a warning, a sound in your chest,
your mouth opening to a word, no

I know. I can't listen to the Beach Boys
without thinking of all the girls they sang to,
& her bubblegum-pink lipstick print
on someone else's mirror, or face.

maybe the difference between remembering
& hurting is just me.

when you deleted & blocked & changed your
Instagram account to private, it was because
your empty hands had nothing left to give,

could only push back,
could only wave goodbye,
could only stop, I know.

I've drawn the curtains. I've screened calls.
I've felt mean & brave, when it didn't matter. when
your heart breaks, every piece is indistinguishable &
the same.

does your pain have a voice? does it need
a space? one last thing I can give: here;
                may you cut your hair & grow it out.
                may no one watch.

                    *- in place of mercy.*
                    by yena sharma purmasir

do you think medusa didn't have to cut loose a serpent or two? shedding those who do nothing but spew malice your way is crucial, even if they end up being the ones you never thought you could live a single moment without. as much as this twists a knife in your gut, you must give yourself permission to do this. how else are you going to make space at your table for the ones who have proven they're actually worthy of sharing your meals with? how else will you learn that you're deserving of being served first, before anyone else?

but you will grow stronger,
grow wiser,
grow the courage to look down and see
yourself in pieces at your own feet.
dare to send your fingers
dancing through the shards
before you pick them up
and call them poetry,
call them a new song,
call them screaming in your car with the windows up

and after you have emptied your throat of
all the pain that finally pulled
itself from your tongue,
you will feel your lungs fill themselves
with the kind of healing that you summoned
all the way from wherever miracles are made.

then you'll breathe it back out
feel it spilling into your story.
you will pour words into your wounds
like salt water,
like the sound of saying what has happened
*can fill the gashes left, courtesy of cruelty.*
and it will, well enough.

and in time, you will find
that while you cannot scrub the scars from your skin
you can rearrange them into something like maps
soft, and webbed, and patiently waiting
for you to trace them
through all your mad, wild mending.

*- one breath at a time.*
by morgan nikola-wren

she said,

     chase the bad memories
     through that cold,
     unfriendly
     wild.

she said,

     chase the bad memories
     through the
     ruins of the
     fallen.

she said,

     chase the bad memories
     until they explode
     & s c a t t er
     to dust.

she said,

     they'll be like
     the stars we still see
     but were burnt out
     before we were born.

*- it will get easier / it will hurt less / give it time.*

sometimes you heal up   & sometimes you
stick out at strange angles
forever..... like an elaborate self-
portrait
drawn by a six year old      & so what? you are
learning what it means to be
the only one

of yourself     & here you are
in all of your glory    in all of your razzmatazz
dramatic lopsided glory
yes:   you are here;   it is morning  ;   you are
wearing heart-
shaped sunglasses   & how grand

it is!   how glamorous & grand ~   to zig & zag
& walk towards home, your body
parting the air
as though parting a beaded curtain

- *untitled II.*
by mckayla robbin

renegade
/'re-ni-gād/
*noun*

> 1: someone who loves themselves
> despite the falsehoods the world
> spills into them.

- & *if you can't love yourself yet, you still
deserve love from others.*

this is for the ones with
starfall hearts and blown glass eyes

this is for the ones with
broken hands and unbroken ties

this is for the ones with
wild hair and ghosts in their lungs

this is for the ones with
unsung mothers and wars on their tongues

this is for the ones with
bruised peach skin and fear-flayed nails

this is for the ones with
hummingbird hearts and thighs that tell tales

of nights they found love and nights to forget
of days passed in silence, words not to regret

- *i am yours.*
by sophia elaine hanson

if you want to put on your very best dancing shoes, then do it. if you want to zip yourself into your golden apple ballgown, then do it. if you want to paint your face while you dream of all the cupid-shaped smudges you'll leave on mirrors for passersby to collect on their lips, then do it. you can do it all & still save yourself & the world for good measure. there's nothing stopping you from being both gentle & valiant, just & magnificent, or any combination you should ever long for. the reason they tell us we cannot have it all is because they fear we will become even more dangerous than we are, & we are already such forces to be reckoned with.

- *open up the wardrobe & step inside.*

(homage to C.S. Lewis's book series
The Chronicles of Narnia)

She carried her hurt around
in a tiny glass jar,
lid tight enough
that it would take
two hands to twist off.

She convinced herself,
that much like Pandora's Box,
opening it would only cause
more harm than good.

It's easier to tell others
that your monsters sleep under your bed
instead of tucked away
in a cold slumber right next to you.

With creatures of the night begging to play,
her mind that was once
an enchanted garden
was becoming a tainted dystopia.

It was only when the
voices rang louder that she began to hear
the soft symphonies of hope
whisper among the madness.
and so she found comfort
in the melodies that the universe
began singing to her.

Slamming her glass jar to the ground
*(what was once a forbidden secret)*
stillness began surrounding her being,
and opening the rim of her mouth,
she began to sing along.

*- a promising ballad.*
by orion carloto

you worry
so much
about
the comfort
of others
that you
cannot
remember
a time
when
you did
something
just
for
yourself.

*- you are worth spoiling.*

When I was a child,
I thought astronauts
and astronomers and anyone who explored the
universe
were space mermaids,

diving into
the unknown ocean of the universe,
our planet the comfortable shore.

This is why lately,
I have stopped asking
the cosmos
for the cure.

To bleed the sad planets out from inside my skin
and replace them with the ashes of happier stars.

It took me nearly three decades to learn how to
embrace
the constellations of my own
tragedies and dive,
courageous, into
the galaxy of who I am,
emerging as the better, stronger version
I deserve myself to be.

When I was a child,
I used to believe anyone
who explored the stars
was a mermaid.

Now that I am grown,
I know that they are.

- *because i am one of them.*
by nikita gill

you did all you could do.
now you must learn
what it means
for you to
live.

*- tweet from august 8th, 2017.*

take my words,

but
expand upon them.
argue with them.
change them.
twist them.

- *make them yours.*

i've
never been

a mirror
nor a lake

for you to
peer

into &
see yourself

or your past
& future paths

reflected
back to you.

*my
story
has never
been
your story.*

*your
story
has never
been my
story.*

*their
story
has never
been anyone
else's story.*

the
wonderment

of all this
can be found

in the
bits & pieces

we're
able to

gather
from

each other
to form

the entire
window.

- *stained glass.*

they will say:

 I. you're not talented enough.
 II. you don't have an original cell in your body.
 III. you don't measure up to the ones who came before you.
 IV. your feelings are shallow.
 V. you're whiny.
 VI. you're a hack.
 VII. you're a whiny hack.
 VIII. none of that could have possibly happened to you.
 IX. . . . but if it did, then you embellished it.
 X. & it's probably your fault anyhow.

*- & you will keep writing anyway.*

soon
they will
have chopped
down all the trees
& with them
all the
b
e
a
u
t
i
f
u
l
w o r d s , s o

*- write the story II.*

nobody
has
the right
to lure
your voice
out of
you—

not
even if
they're
a sea witch
looking
to make
a bargain.

*- rip this page out & keep it with you.*

no
matter
how you choose
to tell your
truths

      *—a whisper*
        *melody*
        *s c r e a m—*

you
are still
toppling
mountain
ranges.

- *you possess avalanches.*

"be
victorious
in
everything
you do.
disturb
the gods,
if that's what
it takes.
& maybe
especially then."

- *mother knows best IV.*

# the rest of this story
## belongs to
## you.

dearest reader,

this is the final poetry collection in my "women are some kind of magic" series. it all started with a princess who collapsed into a pile of ashes & somehow learned to make a queendom from them. that princess-turned-queen was, of course, me. in that first collection, i attempted to summarize the entirety of my life in a little over two hundred pages. everyone i loved. everyone i lost. every struggle. every unsteady step to survival. it seems like an impossible feat & that's because it was. there is & has always been so much more to my story.

it continued, then, with a group of fire witches. the princess had survived & she wanted revenge for everything she'd been put through, especially the sexual violence she had endured & had to watch all around her. messy was the witch. angry was the witch. politically charged was the witch. i allowed her to be all of those things. i allowed *myself* to feel without restriction, without worrying how unladylike everyone would find me. but that witch—that witch-queen—still wasn't ready to share the story she had been keeping behind lock & key for so long.

in a way, that witch & her coven bridged the gap between the princess & the mermaid who had long ago decided to fly far, far away from her problems so she didn't have to deal with them on the page . . . or at all.

finally, that mermaid who had been a witch who had been a queen was ready to tell her story. this tale has been a mix of fantasy & truth for that very reason. i knew the only way i could let the mermaid speak was if she could do it discreetly & safely. i owe that bravery to the #metoo movement, first started by tarana burke. i may never be ready to say the name of the ones who hurt me, but being able to tell the story still lifted the weight from my shoulders. boulders have since been replaced by sea foam.

if there's one thing i hope you take away from this collection, it's that there are so many ways for a victim/survivor to come forward & speak about their experiences with sexual violence. the method i chose doesn't have to be your method, just as your method doesn't have to be my method. it's about what's right for the victim/survivor as an individual. this book, here, was simply the path that was best for me. in the end, all paths are valid &, with any luck, lead to happiness & healing.

may the chorus of mermaids follow you wherever you go. may they offer reassurance whenever you're in need. remember you are one of us. forever. from the glittering sea to the starry skies.

laced with love,
amanda

⌛

coming:
the story you
needed to write
on a bookshelf
waiting to save
someone
else.

# contributors

*in order of appearance*

**lang leav**
author of the foreword
twitter: @langleav
instagram: @langleav
website: langleav.com

**caitlyn siehl**
author of "blade"
twitter: @caitlynsiehl
instagram: @caitlynsiehl
facebook: @caitlynsiehl1

**clementine von radics**
author of "notes on the term survivor"
twitter: @clementinevr
instagram: @clementinevonradics
website: www.clementinevonradicspoet.com

**trista mateer**
author of "untitled"
twitter: @tristamateer
instagram: @tristamateer
website: tristamateer.com

**gretchen gomez**
author of "wading"
twitter: @chicnerdreads
instagram: @chicnerdreads
wordpress: chicnerdreads.wordpress.com

**noor shirazie**
author of "earth / water"
twitter: @shirazien
instagram: @shirazien
facebook: @n00rshirazie
tumblr: @noorshirazie

**jenna clare**
author of "trust me"
twitter: @jennaclarek
instagram: @jennaclarek
website: jennaclarek.com

**ky robinson**
author of "the grit of healing"
twitter: @iamkyrobinson
instagram: @iamkyrobinson
website: kyrobinson.net

**yena sharma purmasir**
author of "in place of mercy"
twitter: @yenapurmasir
instagram: @yenasharmapurmasir
tumblr: @fly-underground

**morgan nikola-wren**
author of "one breath at a time"
twitter: @wrenandink
instagram: @morgannikolawren
website: morgannikolawren.com

**mckayla robbin**
author of "untitled II"
twitter: @bymckayla
instagram: @bymckayla
website: mckaylarobbin.com

**sophia elaine hanson**
author of "i am yours"
twitter: @authorsehanson
instagram: @authorsehanson
tumblr: @sophiaelainehanson
website: sophiaelainehanson.com

**orion carloto**
author of "a promising ballad"
twitter: @orionnichole
instagram: @orionvanessa
youtube: @orionvanessa
website: orioncarloto.com

**nikita gill**
author of "because i am one of them"
twitter: @nktgill
instagram: @nikita_gill

# special acknowledgments

I. *cyrus parker* – you seriously deserve some kind of prize for listening to me rant & rave about this book all these past months, my poet-spouse. most of all, i just want to thank you for letting me spill water & for always being there to help me dry it up. ~O)

II. *christine day* – this was, without question, the most difficult collection i've had to write to date. it went through more drastic changes than all of them combined & kept me up all night for weeks at a time. on the bright side, it was never as difficult as it could have been, all because you were always there for me to turn to.

III. *my contributors* – when i first set out to include poems from other poets i deeply admired, i had no idea how it would go. honestly, this whole thing could have been a disaster. instead, we sang to each other through the uncertain dark, our feet searching for common ground, & it became an accidental masterpiece. thank you for lending me the gorgeous words.

IV. *my family* – to my dad, my stepmom, & my sisters. thank you for coming to every book launch. for reading every word. for desperately asking to read an early copy of each book, even before they're halfway finished. (i'm looking at you, courtney!)

V. *my beta readers* – trista mateer, caitlyn siehl, danika stone, mira kennedy, olivia paez, & alex andrina. from the bottom of my heart: thank you for always pushing me to be the best i can be. thank you for transforming my words. this has been, in no exaggeration, the greatest group effort of a lifetime.

VI. *the people who always make me smile & give me their never-ending support* – gretchen gomez, nikita gill, sophia elaine hanson, iain s. thomas, ky robinson, courtney peppernell, lang leav, shauna sinyard, summer webb, courtney summers, & nicole brinkley. & you, whoever i'm inevitably forgetting.

VII. *my publishing team at andrews mcmeel* – to patty rice, kirsty melville, & holly stayton. there are no words to describe how grateful i am for you & the work that brings my words to life.

VIII. *my readers* – here's to our fourth book. <3

a small space for you to begin your story:

_____
_____
_____
_____
_____
_____
_____
_____
_____

growing up a word-devourer & avid fairy tale lover, it was only natural that amanda lovelace began writing books of her own, & so she did. when she isn't reading or writing, she can be found waiting for pumpkin spice coffee to come back into season & binge-watching *gilmore girls.* (before you ask: team jess all the way.) the lifelong poetess & storyteller currently lives in new jersey with her spouse, their bunnycat, & a combined book collection so large it will soon need its own home. she has her B.A. in english literature with a minor in sociology. her first collection, *the princess saves herself in this one,* won the goodreads choice award for best poetry of 2016 and is a *USA TODAY & Publishers Weekly* bestseller.

 @ladybookmad

@ladybookmad

@amandalovelace

amandalovelace.com

Andrews McMeel Publishing
a division of Andrews McMeel Universal
1130 Walnut Street, Kansas City, Missouri 64106

www.andrewsmcmeel.com

19 20 21 22 23 RR2 10 9 8 7 6 5 4 3 2 1

ISBN: 978-1-4494-9416-2

Library of Congress Control Number: 2018957490

Editor: Patty Rice
Designer: Amanda Lovelace
Art Director: Julie Barnes
Production Editor: David Shaw
Production Manager: Cliff Koehler


ATTENTION: SCHOOLS AND BUSINESSES
Andrews McMeel books are available at quantity discounts with
bulk purchase for educational, business, or sales promotional use.
For information, please e-mail the Andrews McMeel Publishing
Special Sales Department: specialsales@amuniversal.com.